SEP -- 2014

J979.473 NUÑES
Discovering Mission Sa
Clara de Asís /
Nuñes, Sofia.
33341005531107

Z × 10/18 -W
2 × 10/24 W

CALIFORNIA MISSIONS

Discovering Mission Santa Clara de Asís

BY SOFIA NUÑES

Cavendish Square

New York

Published in 2015 by Cavendish Square Publishing, LLC
243 5th Avenue, Suite 136, New York, NY 10016

Copyright © 2015 by Cavendish Square Publishing, LLC

First Edition

No part of this publication may be reproduced, stored in a retrieval system, or transmitted in any form or by any means—electronic, mechanical, photocopying, recording, or otherwise—without the prior permission of the copyright owner. Request for permission should be addressed to Permissions, Cavendish Square Publishing, 243 5th Avenue, Suite 136, New York, NY 10016. Tel (877) 980-4450; fax (877) 980-4454.

Website: cavendishsq.com

This publication represents the opinions and views of the author based on his or her personal experience, knowledge, and research. The information in this book serves as a general guide only. The author and publisher have used their best efforts in preparing this book and disclaim liability rising directly or indirectly from the use and application of this book.

CPSIA Compliance Information: Batch #WS14CSQ

All websites were available and accurate when this book was sent to press.

Library of Congress Cataloging-in-Publication Data

Nuñes, Sofia.
Discovering Mission Santa Clara de Asís / Sofia Nuñes.
pages cm. — (California Missions)
Includes index.
ISBN 978-1-62713-067-7 (hardcover) ISBN 978-1-62713-069-1 (ebook)
1. Santa Clara Mission—History—Juvenile literature. I. Title.

F869.S47M36 2015
979.4'73—dc 3

2014003428

Editorial Director: Dean Miller
Editor: Kristen Susienka
Copy Editor: Cynthia Roby
Art Director: Jeffrey Talbot
Designer: Douglas Brooks
Photo Researcher: J8 Media
Production Manager: Jennifer Ryder-Talbot
Production Editor: David McNamara

The photographs in this book are used by permission and through the courtesy of: Cover photo by JaGa/ Mission Santa Clara.jpg/Wikimedia Commons; Eugene Zelenko/File: USA-Santa Clara-Mission-3.jpg/Wikimedia Commons, 1; Nagel Photography/Shutterstock.com, 4; Ann Thiermann/Dancing at Quiroste/Ann Thiermann, 8; Buyenlarge/Archive Photos/ Getty Images, 10; © 2012 Pentacle Press, 11; © 2014 Pentacle Press, 13; Steve Heap/Shutterstock.com, 14; De Agostini/Getty Images, 17; Preservapedia/Adobe bricks drying in front of the Presidio chapel.jpg/Wikimedia Commons, 19; Camazine Scott/Photo Researchers/Getty Images, 22; North Wind Picture Archives/Alamy, 24; © North Wind/North Wind Picture Archives, 26; Unknown/hb-7-1-001A.tif/Santa Clara University Library, 28; Universal Images Group/SuperStock, 30; Everett Collection/ SuperStock, 32; Science & Society Picture Library/Contributor/SSPL/Getty Images, 31; © 2012 Pentacle Press, 33; Nagel Photography/Shutterstock.com, 34; Panoramic Images/Getty Images, 36; JaGa/Mission Santa Clara.jpg/Wikimedia Commons, 41.

Printed in the United States of America

CALIFORNIA
MISSIONS

Contents

Mission Santa Clara de Asís was built and
decorated by the men, women, and children
who lived there.

4

1
Exploring a New World

Before the Gold Rush in 1848, California had few visitors. Its primary inhabitants were **indigenous people**, who lived in hundreds of different tribes up and down the coast. Their lives were changed dramatically by the arrival of Spanish colonists. The Spanish had arrived in what is now Mexico, and they wanted to expand their control up the coast of California. They decided to build a chain of missions along the coast.

A mission is a place where people teach others about a certain religion and other aspects of a foreign way of life or culture. The first California mission was built in 1769. By 1823, there were twenty-one missions along the coast of California, stretching from San Diego to Sonoma.

NEW SPAIN

The 1400s and 1500s were a time when Europeans explored places all over the world. European governments were eager to find riches and search for more land. Spain was one of the first countries in Europe to make exploration a priority. Some Spanish explorers conquered entire populations in what is now Mexico. The Spanish named their conquered land **New Spain**.

Soon, Spanish explorers would sail north from New Spain up and down the **Alta California** and **Baja California** coasts. *Alta* in Spanish means "upper," and refers to the land that is now part of the state of California. "Lower," or *Baja* California, refers to the land below it, reaching into Mexico. From these explorations, Spain hoped to expand its empire around the globe.

CABRILLO AND VIZCAÍNO

In 1542, Juan Rodríguez Cabrillo became the first Spanish explorer sent from New Spain to explore the west coast of North America. His goal was to find a river that joined the Pacific and Atlantic Oceans, though he was unsuccessful in his task.

In 1602, Spanish explorer Sebastián Vizcaíno was sent to continue Cabrillo's search. Based on Vizcaíno's records, there he and his crew met the Ohlone, a tribe of Native people of California. Less than 200 years later, the descendants of these Ohlone would build Mission Santa Clara de Asís.

Vizcaíno returned to New Spain, also unsuccessful. The **viceroy** did not think it was worthwhile to invest the time and money in future explorations. No Spanish ships sailed to California for the next 160 years.

In the 1700s, Russia and England sent ships to the Pacific Coast of North America and built settlements. Because of this, Spain worried that it would lose the land that Cabrillo and Vizcaíno had claimed. The government decided to take measures to permanently control Alta California, starting with the Native people living there.

2
The
Ohlone

Centuries before the first Europeans arrived on California's coast, or Catholic **friars** (called *frays* in Spanish) began plans to build missions, many different Native American tribes were already living there. The Ohlone tribe lived in the area near where Santa Clara de Asís would be built.

There were many Ohlone, spreading from the San Francisco area to south of Monterey Bay. It was not unusual for members of tribes living within a few miles of each other to speak different languages. They had no written form of communication.

The Ohlone hunted for food, searching for deer, antelope, ducks, and geese. The Ohlone also made boats to access the abundant seafood from the ocean, and gathered berries, mushrooms, grass seeds, and other plants they found growing in the area.

One of the Ohlone's most important food staples was acorns. There were different types of acorns growing in the northern region of Alta California, and the tribe took advantage of them all. The Ohlone ground the acorns into flour, which was then used to make porridge, biscuits, and soup.

VILLAGE STRUCTURE

Every village had an assembly house and a *temescal*, or sweathouse. The assembly house was made of **tule**, which was a mat of tightly woven reeds used to block out rain and wind. This building was used for large gatherings and could hold the entire village population. The temescal was a small hut used by members of the tribe to cleanse their bodies through sweating. Temescals are similar to today's saunas. The Ohlone went through this ritual for many reasons, such as healing an illness, curing a skin disease, or preparing for a hunt or religious ceremony. Individual homes for the Ohlone were constructed from wooden posts and were covered with tule.

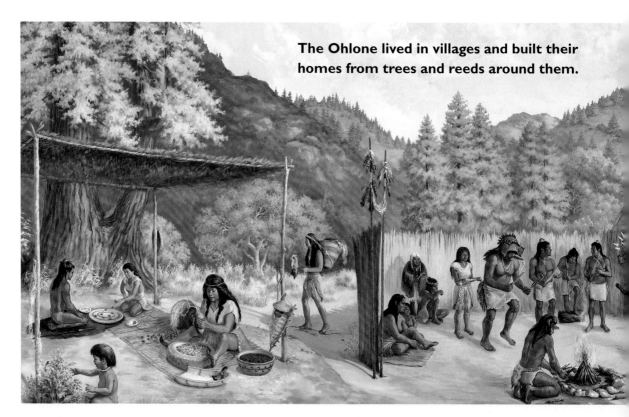

The Ohlone lived in villages and built their homes from trees and reeds around them.

The chief, who could be either male or female, was one of the wealthiest members of the village. The chief's wealth was used for the benefit of the entire village and those in need. Whenever a visitor came to the village, it was the responsibility of the chief to feed him well and give him gifts. The chief also led hunts for food.

The elderly members of the Ohlone tribe were treated with great respect. When they had something to say, the younger people listened carefully. The chief made sure the elderly were cared for and had food and shelter.

Children were raised not just by their mothers and fathers, but also by the extended family, including aunts, uncles, and grandparents. Children had lots of time to play and enjoy their natural surroundings.

HUNTING, GATHERING, AND HARD WORK

Ohlone men were skilled hunters. Their most prized possessions were the bows they crafted by hand. A hunter could take ten days to perfect his bow. Arrowheads fashioned from rocks and a natural glass called obsidian were shaped by hand. All weapons and tools were made from wood, stones, shells, or animal bones.

Ohlone women were equally gifted in basket weaving. They made beautiful baskets that were woven tightly enough to hold water. Some are exhibited in different museums and libraries around the world today. These handwoven baskets were a necessity for the Ohlone, as baskets were used for almost every daily chore. Women used the baskets to shake and separate seeds from plants, to carry and store water, to cook food, and to carry almost any load.

Many Native groups wove strong baskets to help them carry items and water.

When the Spanish arrived and built missions on the land, the Ohlone lifestyle changed forever. Before the Spanish came to California, however, they had changed the lives of many Native Americans living in Baja California, the place of the first mission systems.

3
The
Mission System

In the mid-1700s, Spanish rulers set out a plan to colonize California. There were three branches to each settlement. These were the missions, the *presidios*, and the *pueblos*.

The Catholic missions, which were the religious branch, were to be built first to attract the local peoples. Some Californians joined the missions voluntarily. However, many Ohlone were forced to leave their villages against their will and live on the mission sites.

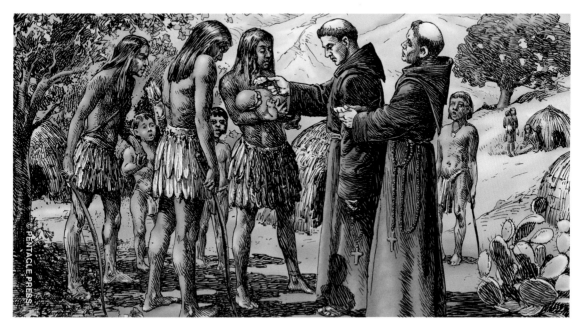

Friars baptized neophytes and their children into the Catholic faith.

The people who came to the mission were taught trades to help keep the mission running smoothly. The missionaries taught the indigenous people about Christianity and then baptized them. **Baptism** is a ritual that is preformed when someone is accepted into the **Christian** faith. Once the indigenous Californians were baptized into the Catholic faith, they were called **neophytes**.

The Spanish also built presidios along the coast. Presidios were military forts for the soldiers. Each presidio's function was to house soldiers who would protect the Spanish settlers of the mission, watch over the neophytes at the mission, and enforce Spanish laws.

The Spanish also developed pueblos, or agricultural towns, in the fertile valleys outside the missions. The purpose of the pueblos was to supply the presidios with grain and other staples which, at that time, were being shipped from Mexico. In this way, the settlements would become more self-sufficient.

Keeping in mind that the Spanish missionaries estimated it would take ten years to establish each settlement, the Spanish government made long-range plans for the California coast. They planned to create a mission in the south (San Diego), and in the north (Monterey) of Alta California. More missions would be built between these missions. As they were built, they formed *El Camino Real,* a road that stretches 600 miles (965 kilometers) along California's coast. Its name means "The Royal Road."

However, to expand their empire and build a new land, the Spanish needed more than a well-developed plan. They needed indigenous Californians like the Ohlone. With only two missionaries and five or six soldiers per mission, the neophytes' labor was necessary in order to build the missions and keep them running. The goal was for the neophytes to eventually be able to run the missions on their own. Spanish rulers assumed that the neophytes would become loyal Spanish citizens, thus expanding the Spanish empire even farther. During this time, the Spanish soldiers and missionaries continued to establish more missions in other areas. It was the hope that eventually the Ohlone would be left to live on their own as new Spanish citizens. The mission would then be ruled by the government, rather than the church.

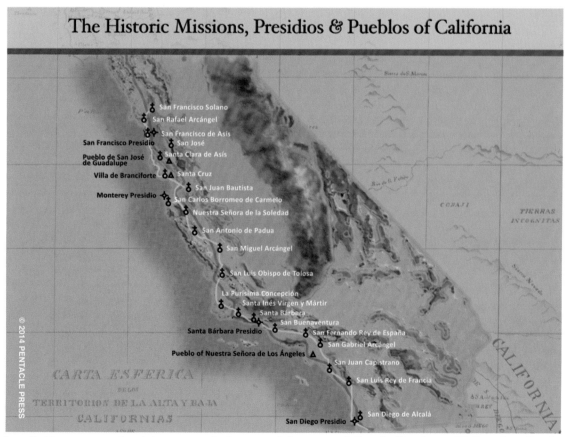

In all, there were twenty-one missions and four presidios built along **El Camino Real** (illustrated by the yellow line).

Fray Junípero Serra was the first leader of the Alta California mission system.

4
From Spain to Monterey Bay

While the mission would not have succeeded without the many Native American men, women, and children that lived and worked at Mission Santa Clara de Asís, there were a few key figures who also played important roles in the founding of the Santa Clara de Asís mission.

FOUNDER FRAY JUNÍPERO SERRA

Fray Junípero Serra, known as the founder of the California mission system, was part of the **Franciscan** order in Majorca, Spain. The monks of this order are called Franciscans because they live by the Christian example set by Saint Francis of Assisi. When a person joins the Franciscan brotherhood, he takes a vow never to marry, never to seek material wealth, and always to act in total obedience to the Christian god. In Serra's time, Franciscans wore gray woolen robes tied at the waist with a piece of white rope. Their feet were bare except for sandals.

Once he became a priest, Fray Serra remained in Majorca and taught classes in theology. In 1749, he and two of his former students, Fray Francisco Palóu and Fray Juan Crespí, were offered the chance to follow their dreams of **missionary** work. A missionary travels to foreign lands teaching people about Christianity in an effort to **convert** them. Catholic friars were needed as missionaries in New Spain. Although the site was thousands of miles from home and they would probably never see Majorca again, they enthusiastically boarded a ship for the long journey. Serra was determined to share his religion with the Native Californians, people who didn't know about Christianity.

THE MISSIONARIES REACH NEW SPAIN

Once Serra, Palóu, and Crespí arrived in the port city of Veracruz, New Spain, they still had close to 269 miles (433 km) to go before reaching Mexico City. The three missionaries spent about fourteen days traveling to reach the College of San Fernando in Mexico City. They chose to walk this distance instead of riding mules because they wanted to learn about the land and the people. Once Serra arrived in Mexico City in January 1750, he spent the next seventeen years fulfilling various duties at the College of San Fernando.

REACHING BAJA CALIFORNIA AND ALTA CALIFORNIA

In 1767, Fray Serra was chosen to supervise the fifteen existing Spanish missions in Baja California, which is today northwestern Mexico. Serra worked hard to keep the Franciscan missionaries happy. He tried to visit each mission at least once each year to make sure the friars had everything they needed. A year later, when Spain decided to strengthen its claim on Alta California, Serra was the best candidate to head up new missions in the uncharted area. He became involved in the founding of the first nine California missions, though explorers such as Gaspár de Portolá and Captain Don Juan Bautista de Anza helped him choose the actual sites.

GASPÁR DE PORTOLÁ

In 1769, the viceroy of New Spain appointed Gaspár de Portolá to lead a group to establish settlements in Alta California. Portolá sent three ships and two walking expeditions to San Diego. Fray

Soldiers and friars built their presidios and missions on large pieces of land belonging to Native communities.

Serra accompanied Portolá in one of the land groups, which left in March 1769. On July 16, 1769, Fray Serra founded California's first mission, Mission San Diego de Alcalá. This was to be the first permanent European settlement in California.

As Serra and his companions planned new mission sites, they looked for areas with plenty of fresh water, fertile soil for planting crops and feeding livestock, and a supply of wood for building structures and furniture.

Most importantly, the area needed to be inhabited by large groups of indigenous people. The missionaries wanted to be near tribes in order to teach them about Christianity. They also needed the Native Americans to help them build the mission and do all the chores to maintain the mission's productivity and success.

DON JUAN BAUTISTA DE ANZA EXPLORES FURTHER

In 1774, Spain sent Captain Don Juan Bautista de Anza to further investigate the California coast. After his small-scale initial trek along the coast in January 1774, Anza hurried back to Mexico City to plan a larger trip. He wanted to reach San Francisco Bay and bring a large group of people along to settle the area.

Anza's journey began in October 1775 when he set off with about 240 people—settlers, soldiers, and Franciscan friars. They reached Monterey in March. Many people stayed there, while he and a Catholic friar went farther north to select sites for a presidio. They chose mission sites around San Francisco Bay, including the land where Mission Santa Clara de Asís would be built.

5
The Early Days

Led by Frays José Murguía and Tomás de la Peña, the founding ceremony for Mission Santa Clara de Asís was held two years after Don Juan Bautista de Anza located the site. On January 12, 1777, the founders arrived at the site of Santa Clara de Asís. Peña constructed a small, sheltered altar and held the mission's first Mass under an arbor of branches. A wooden cross was also built and hammered into the soil to mark the site. Santa Clara de Asís was the

Adobe bricks were important to building each mission and presidio; they would be left to dry in the sun until hard enough to be used for building.

first mission to be named after a female saint. Santa Clara, or Saint Claire, had been an early and devout follower of Saint Francis.

The friars prepared a report, called an *informé*, of everything they had received from New Spain and the other nearby missions to help the Santa Clara de Asís mission get started. From this informé we know that the friars started out with two plowshares, four crowbars, thirty-six hoes, twelve digging sticks, twenty-four axes, twelve machetes, twelve sickles, and four plows. Every mission also had a *carreta*, which was a two-wheeled cart, pulled by oxen.

Original reports show that the Santa Clara de Asís mission was also given four hogs, twenty hens, and three roosters, along with cattle, sheep, goats, pigs, *burros*, horses, and mules. The tools would help them to build the mission, while the livestock, or animals, would be an important source of food for a growing community. Mission Santa Clara de Asís seemed to have everything it needed, but it was still missing one major component. It was missing the participation of the local population, the Ohlone.

THE BUILDINGS OF SANTA CLARA DE ASÍS

The church was one of the first buildings to be constructed. The other buildings were built in the shape of a **quadrangle** connected to the church, forming a courtyard in the middle. The Santa Clara de Asís mission had living quarters for the Catholic missionaries, a dining room, and workrooms for weaving cloth, tanning hide, and other trades. There were dormitory-type rooms for unmarried boys, and a separate place for unmarried girls, called a *monjerío*.

The missionaries needed the help of the Ohlone for the actual building of the structures. They enticed them to work by offering food, glass beads, blankets, and other trade goods. The more the Ohlone helped, the more gifts they received. Under the Catholic friars' supervision, the Ohlone built the first church and living quarters of wood and thatch.

THE OHLONE CONVERT

One of the main reasons why the area around Santa Clara de Asís was such a great place for a mission was the large population of Ohlone nearby. Initially, however, the friars at Mission Santa Clara de Asís had a difficult time persuading the Ohlone to join the mission. Some Ohlone hindered the missions by stealing livestock. The soldiers from the presidio punished and killed several people who stole from the missions. The violence of the soldiers discouraged many from interacting with their new neighbors. Overall, however, the local people were friendly to the Spanish, but kept their distance.

In May, several months after arriving and soon after the church was built, something terrible happened which changed the Ohlone's view of the friars. Disease swept through a nearby village, killing many of the Ohlone children. When the friars heard of the widespread sickness, they went to the Ohlone villages to help. The friars knew they could treat some of the children and make them better. They also believed that those who were too sick to survive should be baptized, as this was the only way the friars believed the Ohlone could go to Heaven. Spanish soldiers brought the sick children to the mission to care for them, and many of their parents came, too. These families were some of the first Ohlone to become neophytes at Mission Santa Clara de Asís.

As the Ohlone became comfortable at the mission site, the friars encouraged them to be baptized into the Christian faith. The missionaries also emphasized the beautiful Catholic ceremonies and music. The Ohlone had enjoyed dancing and singing in their religion. This helped encourage the Ohlone to adopt Christianity. Despite its slow start, the mission recorded the most baptisms of any California mission, with 8,536 baptisms between the years 1777 and 1832.

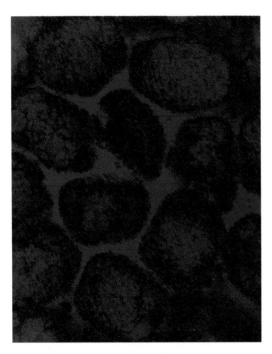

Epidemics of smallpox (magnified here) and other diseases greatly reduced populations at each mission.

Once the Ohlone were baptized and became neophytes, they were not allowed to practice their old religion. The neophytes were told that they must live at the mission, although occasionally they might be allowed to visit their old villages. Understandably, many neophytes did not like this rule, or any of the rules that were imposed on them.

6
Daily Life at Santa Clara de Asís

Like at other missions, daily life at Mission Santa Clara de Asís varied little from day to day. The ringing of one of Santa Clara de Asís's bells alerted everyone to the day's schedule. Each of the California missions had at least two bells—it is believed that one bell rang for work, mealtimes, and rest, while another bell rang when it was time to pray or have devotionals, which are short religious services.

The Ohlone had never lived such a structured lifestyle. They were used to working when they needed to work and sleeping when they needed to rest. The missions changed that.

Shortly after sunrise, everyone went to the mission church to pray and sing. An hour later, the bell rang for breakfast. The rest of the day usually went like this: neophytes labored at many tasks, such as weaving, farming, tanning leather, and making tools in order to keep the mission running.

As with the other missions, gardening and farming were critical to the mission's survival. Mission Santa Clara de Asís boasted healthy, ripe crops of peaches, apricots, apples, pears, figs, and grapes. Even though the grapevines did not grow as well as the other crops, the wine produced from the grapes was considered good.

Daily life at all the missions involved working, praying, and learning.

Sometimes an expert in a particular field was brought in to help teach the neophytes a trade. In 1792, Miguel Sangrado, a tanner and shoemaker, came to Santa Clara de Asís. He helped guide neophytes in the tanning of 2,000 hides that year. To tan hides, the workers first had to scrape every bit of meat off of them. Then the workers would hang the hides on posts or stretch them and lay them out on the ground to dry. Once dry, they were sold to traders.

Neophyte women wove baskets as they had done when they lived in their villages. They also learned to weave blankets from wool. They made white woolen blankets with yellow stripes. While most dyes used at the missions were imported, the yellow color supposedly came from wildflowers native to the area.

As the years passed and the growth of the mission's population slowed, many neophytes were given the task of recruiting other Native Californians into the mission system. Some Santa Clara de Asís neophytes headed to the nearby pueblo of San

José to find new converts. Others returned to their old Ohlone villages or to other tribes miles away to bring back new people to convert. Often these new converts were brought to the mission against their will. Many neophytes quickly tired of the mission and longed for their old way of life. Some even tried to leave the mission and escape to their own villages. Soldiers were sent to bring back these neophytes. The neophytes were then beaten, jailed, or locked in shackles.

A Life of Structure

An average day at Mission Santa Clara followed this schedule:

6:00 A.M.	The mission bells rang to wake everyone at the mission and at the ranchería.
6:01 A.M.	Time for prayers.
6:30 A.M.	Breakfast.
7:00 A.M.	The bells rang to call everyone to work.
12:00 P.M.	Lunch.
1:00 P.M.	A rest period, called a *siesta*.
3:00 P.M.	Everyone returned to work.
5:00 P.M.	Dinner.
6:00 P.M.	Evening prayers.
7:00 P.M.	Free time.
8:00 P.M.	Bedtime for women.
9:00 P.M.	Bedtime for men.

The neophytes who worked hard to please the missionaries were free from harm. The younger Ohlone who had been raised within the mission system knew of no other life outside the white-walled church and its quadrangle. They didn't know about the days of fishing in the ocean or spending afternoons picking acorns or berries. The young did, however, hear grumbles from the older neophytes about their dissatisfaction with mission life. As the negative talk grew, so did the discontent among young and old alike. As the years passed, many Ohlone neophytes became more and more unhappy with their situation.

DAILY DUTIES OF A MISSIONARY

It was the friars' responsibility to educate the neophytes in the Catholic religion and the Spanish language. They led the young children in studies each morning and afternoon while the adults worked.

While the friars never personally received any money for the work the Native Americans did, they had to make sure everyone knew a trade in order to keep the mission running well. If the mission did not bring in enough money to support itself, it would be in danger of closing. The missionaries sometimes beat the neophytes who did not do their jobs, or when possible, had the soldiers punish them. This sparked tension and led to troubles later on.

7
Obstacles at Santa Clara de Asís

The original church of Mission Santa Clara de Asís was founded on the banks of the Guadalupe River. This was the first of five different sites for this mission. Within two years of the founding, the first church was flooded, and the missionaries were forced to move. They quickly constructed a temporary church while the mission compound was being built out of **adobe**.

It took time to make adobe buildings. The friars had to teach the neophytes how to mix mud with clay and straw. Then the mixture had to be put into molds and dried in the sun.

Fray Serra was present for the laying of the cornerstone of the third church in 1781. The church took two and a half years to complete. This third church contained the first painted decorations mentioned in records about this mission, though no details were given as to its design. When it was finished, Mission Santa Clara de Asís was known as one of the most beautiful missions in all of California.

Unfortunately, after earthquakes in 1812 and 1818 destroyed the church, the missionaries were forced to move the church a fourth time. Again, this was a temporary site until the fifth church and connecting structures were completed in 1825.

There were six different churches built at Mission Santa Clara. Here, the fifth church is still standing, but it was later destroyed by a terrible fire.

The fifth church was ornately decorated, with a ceiling designed by the Mexican artist Agustín Dávila. At many missions, the neophytes painted scenes and designs on the walls, but Dávila was brought to Santa Clara de Asís specifically to design the ceiling of the new mission church. Dávila had help from the neophytes, who helped him paint under his guidance.

The fifth church remained in good condition until 1926, when an early morning fire swept through its walls, burning it to the ground. The sixth and final church was built in the same spot, but this time the church was made of concrete to protect it from burning again. The beautifully painted ceiling was also destroyed in the fire, but a copy was made in the new church following the original design.

Natural disasters in the area, including floods, earthquakes, and fires, caused Mission Santa Clara de Asís to be built six times in five different locations. However, it was trouble between the missionaries, Ohlone, and nearby settlers that caused strife at the mission.

SAN JOSÉ

In 1777, the year that Mission Santa Clara de Asís was founded, the pueblo of San José was also started by the Spanish. The pueblo was a farming community formed to strengthen the Spanish presence on the coast. From the very beginning, the people of the pueblo of San José and the residents of Mission Santa Clara de Asís did not get along. They argued primarily over land and water rights for their crops and livestock. Sometimes the livestock of the two groups mixed, which led to more disagreements. Eventually, they set up boundaries to separate the pastures where the animals roamed.

One of the missionaries who served at Mission Santa Clara de Asís, Fray Magín de Catalá, tried to draw the pueblo of San José and the Santa Clara de Asís mission together by building a four-mile (6.4-km) road from the pueblo to the mission's church doors. Neophytes planted willow trees all along the road to provide shade and protect people from wild cattle. It took 200 workers to finish building the road.

When it was complete, the road was called the *Alameda*. The road did not bring very many San José residents to Santa Clara de Asís, but it was a beautiful road that was used for decades. It has since been expanded and most of the trees have been replaced. After a few years tensions between the pueblo and the mission fizzled, but most of the occupants at the pueblo of San José never became friendly with those at the Santa Clara de Asís mission.

San José was a quiet, small town until the Gold Rush in 1848. It then became the first state capital of California in 1849 and

Despite having the same name, the pueblo of San Jose and Mission San Jose were not located near each other.

remained so until 1852. The city has continued to grow, and today it is home to San José State University, the first state college in California, which was established in 1857.

THE OHLONE FALL TO DISEASE

One of the biggest problems for the entire mission system, as well as Mission Santa Clara de Asís, was the threat of disease for the Native Californians. When the Spanish arrived, they brought illnesses such as measles, smallpox, pneumonia, and mumps. The Ohlone and other tribes had never been exposed to these diseases. When they came in contact with them, thousands of tribe members died because they did not have any immunity. In fact, it is estimated that the indigenous Californian population decreased from 300,000 in the 1760s to 30,000 by 1850. Through all the hardship, the Ohlone persisted. Many descendants live on today.

8
Secularization

In 1810, Spain owned all the missions and the land surrounding them. During that same year, New Spain revolted against Spain and fought a long civil war. In 1821, after eleven years of fighting, New Spain became its own country—Mexico.

MEXICO CLAIMS THE MISSIONS

Members of the Mexican government wanted the rich mission lands for themselves. They planned to send more people north to settle the area and make their country stronger. Government officials planned to secularize the missions, taking some land for these new immigrants to live on and turning over other areas of land to its original inhabitants, the Ohlone. This would mean taking the missions away from the Franciscan friars and replacing them with parish

By the mid-1800s Mexico controlled much of the land in the West.

31

priests, who would perform church services, but would not be in charge of the mission lands or neophytes.

The Spanish missionaries, who would lose power over their land and their missions, were strongly against **secularization**. The friars had changed the life of the Ohlone, a self-sufficient culture that had lived undisturbed for centuries or more, into a group that had become dependent on the mission system for its livelihood. They believed that the neophytes were not ready to operate the mission lands on their own.

While Mexico's original intention of secularization was to turn much of the missions' land over to the Ohlone, this did not happen. In April 1834, Mexican governor José Figueroa began secularizing

Hundreds of years after the Spanish first sailed to California, the missions were secularized.

Neophytes that left the mission struggled to survive.

the missions. Governor Figueroa did not plan to give the valuable land back to the neophytes. He expected the Native Americans to continue working in the mission fields, but they would not own them. Instead, the land would belong to the government.

Mission Santa Clara de Asís was secularized in 1837, and its buildings were left to fall apart. The neophytes left the mission, leaving no one to take care of the structures, the crops, or the animals.

The Ohlone who had lived at Mission Santa Clara de Asís were lost without the mission system. Those who tried to return to their villages found problems they'd never experienced. They couldn't hunt game because the livestock from the mission had driven the wild animals away. The Ohlone couldn't gather grass seed or acorns because the sheep and cattle had eaten the grass, and the oak trees, where acorns once grew abundantly, had been cut for fuel and to make furniture and other materials.

The original cross used at the dedication ceremony in 1777 remains outside Mission Santa Clara today.

9
The Mission Today

The United States went to war with Mexico in 1846. After two years of fighting, the war ended and Mexico was forced to sell 500,000 square miles (1,300,000 sq km) of land, including Alta California, to the United States. In 1850 California became the 31st state in the Union. The following year, an American **Jesuit** priest named John Nobili came to the mission to fix the buildings and create the first college in California. This gave the eighth mission a whole new purpose in the development of California.

In March 1851, the doors of Santa Clara College were opened. In 1912, the college was renamed Santa Clara University. Today, this university is still an institution for higher education, and Mission Santa Clara de Asís sits in its center. It is the only mission of all of the original twenty-one California missions to be a part of a United States college campus.

If you walk around the campus of Santa Clara University today, you can see the adobe lodge and adobe wall, the only parts of the original buildings that survived the 1926 fire. Restored in 1981, they are the oldest buildings on campus. The front of the mission church features the original wooden cross of 1777 that was planted at its founding. It is now covered in

Today Mission Santa Clara is part of Santa Clara University and will always have a place in California's history.

redwood to protect it. Services are still held in the church.

Around the campus, visitors can find grinding stones and 170-year-old olive trees, which take them back to the days of a thriving, fruitful mission.

Although the mission system was meant to educate the indigenous people of California about Spanish life and beliefs, it had a much different outcome. Instead, the mission system transformed Native American lifestyles that had been lived for thousands of years. However, the missions did bring a new culture to the land, and helped make California what it is today. Many farming techniques and architectural designs are still around and practiced, thanks to the work begun by the Spanish and the Ohlone. Without the missions, California would be a very different place today.

10
Make Your Own Mission Model

To make your own model of Mission Santa Clara de Asís, you will need:

- Foam Core board
- ruler
- X-ACTO® knife (ask for an adult's help)
- paintbrush
- brown, cream, red, and green paint
- Scotch tape
- glue
- paper (white)
- toothpicks
- miniature gold bell
- decorative flowers and leaves (greenery)
- Styrofoam crosses

DIRECTIONS

Adult supervision is suggested.

Step 1: Cut a large Foam Core board to measure 42" × 30" (106.6 cm × 76.2 cm) for your base. Paint it green. Let dry.

42"

30"

Step 2: Cut two pieces of Foam Core board with the dimensions shown. These are the front and back of the church. Cut a window as shown in the front.

Step 3: Cut a piece of Foam Core with the dimensions 18.5" × 7" (47 cm × 17.8 cm). This is the right side of the church.

Step 4: Cut another piece of Foam Core to measure 18.5" × 10" (47 cm × 25.4 cm). This is the left side of the church.

Step 5: Cut a piece of Foam Core that is 18.5" × 3" (47 × 7.6 cm). This is the right side of the bell tower.

Step 6: Cut two pieces of Foam Core for the church extension with the dimensions shown here.

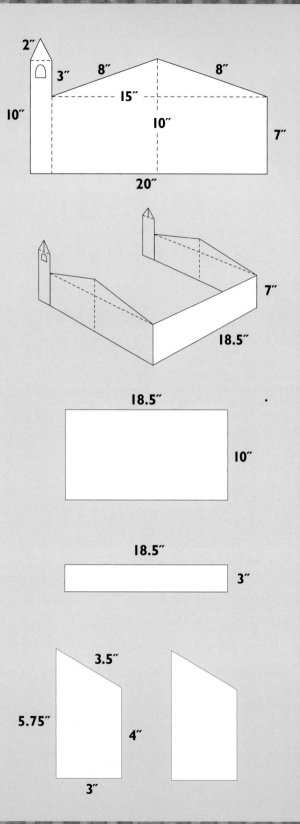

Step 7: For the extension wall, cut a piece of Foam Core to measure 10" × 4" (25.4 cm × 10.2 cm) and attach. Paint all walls with cream-colored paint. Let dry. Tape and glue the inside edges of all church walls together. Then, attach the extension walls at the front of the church and halfway back on the right side of the wall.

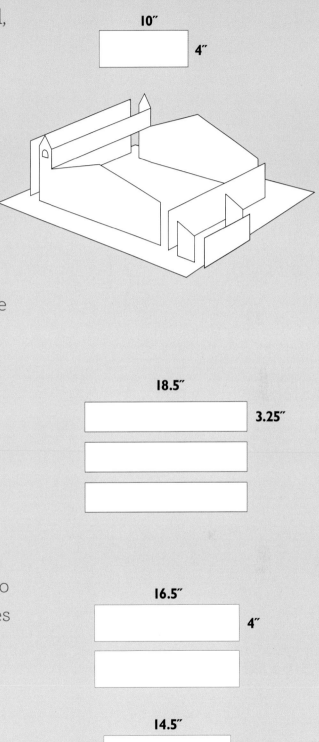

Step 8: Make the outer courtyard walls by cutting three pieces of Foam Core to measure 18.5" × 3.25" (47 cm × 8.3 cm). These will be the outside walls. Paint with cream-colored paint.

Step 9: To make the inner two courtyard walls, cut two pieces of Foam Core to measure 16.5" × 4" (41.9 cm × 10.2 cm). Cut a courtyard wall (inside wall) to measure 14.5" × 4" (36.8 cm × 10.2 cm).

Step 10: Attach the courtyard walls to the church as shown.

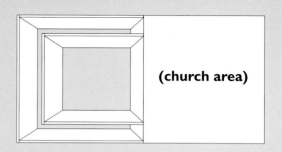

(church area)

Step 11: To make the church roof, cut a piece of paper 19" × 16.5" (48.3 cm × 42 cm). Paint this red.

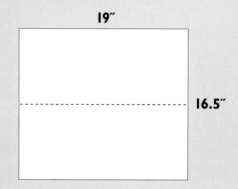

19"

16.5"

Step 12: Make the bell tower roof by cutting a piece of white paper 19" × 4.5" (48.3 cm × 11.4 cm). For the extension roof, cut a piece of paper to measure 10" x 4" (25.4 cm × 10.2 cm).

19"

4.5"

10"

4"

Step 13: For the courtyard roofs, cut three pieces of paper measuring 18.5" × 3" (47 cm × 7.6 cm). Paint these red.

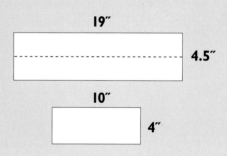

18.5"

3.25"

Step 14: Glue the roofs to the buildings.

Step 15: Slide a toothpick through a miniature bell and insert into bell tower window. Decorate the mission with greenery and Styrofoam crosses.

Use this as a reference for your mission.

Key Dates in Mission History

1492   Christopher Columbus reaches the West Indies

1542   Cabrillo's expedition to California

1602   Sebastián Vizcaíno sails to California

1713   Fray Junípero Serra is born

1769   Founding of San Diego de Alcalá

1770   Founding of San Carlos Borroméo del Río Carmelo

1771   Founding of San Antonio de Padua and San Gabriel Arcángel

1772   Founding of San Luis Obispo de Tolosa

1775–76   Founding of San Juan Capistrano

1776   Founding of San Francisco de Asís

1776   Declaration of Independence is signed

1777	Founding of Santa Clara de Asís
1782	Founding of San Buenaventura
1784	Fray Serra dies
1786	Founding of Santa Bárbara
1787	Founding of La Purísima Concepción
1791	Founding of Santa Cruz and Nuestra Señora de la Soledad
1797	Founding of San José, San Juan Bautista, San Miguel Arcángel, and San Fernando Rey de España
1798	Founding of San Luis Rey de Francia
1804	Founding of Santa Inés
1817	Founding of San Rafael Arcángel
1823	Founding of San Francisco Solano
1833	Mexico passes Secularization Act
1848	Gold found in northern California
1850	California becomes the thirty-first state

Glossary

adobe (uh-DOH-bee) Sun-dried bricks made of straw, mud, and sometimes manure.

Alta California (AL-tuh ka-luh-FOR-nyuh) The mission area today known as the state of California.

Baja California (BAH-ha ka-luh-FOR-nyuh) The Mexican peninsula directly south of the state of California.

baptism (BAP-tih-zum) A sacrament marked by ritual use of water that makes someone a member of a Christian community and cleanses the person of his or her sins.

Christian (KRIS-chun) Someone who follows the Christian religion, or the teachings of Jesus Christ and the Bible.

convert (kun-VERT) To change religious beliefs.

Franciscan (fran-SIS-kin) A member of a Catholic religious group started by Saint Francis of Assisi in 1209.

friar (FRY-ur) A brother in a communal religious order. Friars can also be priests.

indigenous people (in-DIJ-en-us PEA-pel) People native born to a particular region or environment.

Jesuit (JEH-zoo-it) A member of the Roman Catholic Society of Jesus devoted to missionary and educational work.

missionary (MIH-shuh-nayr-ee) A person who teaches his or her religion to people who have different beliefs.

neophyte (NEE-uh-fyt) A person who has converted to another religion; Greek for "new converted."

New Spain (NOO SPAYN)
The area where the Spanish colonists had their capital in North America and that would later become Mexico.

quadrangle (KWAH-drayn-gul) The mission buildings that form a square around a central courtyard.

secularization (seh-kyoo-luh-rih-ZAY-shun) A process by which the mission lands were made to be nonreligious.

tule (TOO-lee) Reeds used by Native Americans to help build their homes.

viceroy (VYS-roy) A government official who rules an area as a representative of the king.

Pronunciation Guide

carreta (kah-RAY-tah)

fray (FRAY)

informé (in-for-MAAY)

monjerío (mohn-hay-REE-oh)

Ohlone (oh-LOH-nee)

pueblos (PWAY-blohz)

siesta (see-EHS-tuh)

temescal (teh-mes-kal)

Find Out More

To learn more about the California missions, check out these books, websites, and museums:

BOOKS

Genet, Donna. *Father Junípero Serra: Founder of the California Missions.* Springfield, NJ: Enslow Publishers, 1996.

Kuska, George and Barbara Linse. *Our Mission Past for Kids.* Los Osos, CA: EZ Nature Books, 2004.

White, Tekla. *San Francisco Bay Area Missions.* Minneapolis, MN: Lerner Publishing, 2008.

Williams, Jack S. *The Ohlone of California.* New York, NY: PowerKids Press, 2003.

WEBSITES

California Mission Foundation

www.californiamissionfoundation.org

This website provides quick and easy facts on the missions and the organization that preserves and protects the missions today.

California Missions Resource Center

www.missionscalifornia.com

This website provides essential facts about each mission, as well as a timeline and a photo gallery.

Ohlone Nation

www.ohlonenation.org

This website details the history of the Ohlone Nation in their own words. It also provides information about the tribe today and events taking place throughout the year.

San Diego History Center

www.sandiegohistory.org/journal/69fall/struggle.htm

This website is part of the San Diego History Center. It provides articles from its magazine, *The Journal of San Diego History*, including articles about the missions.

MUSEUMS

De Saisset Museum
500 El Camino Real
Santa Clara, California 95050
(408) 554-4528

Index

Page numbers in **boldface** are illustrations.